Rundlett Middle School

P9-CCX-501

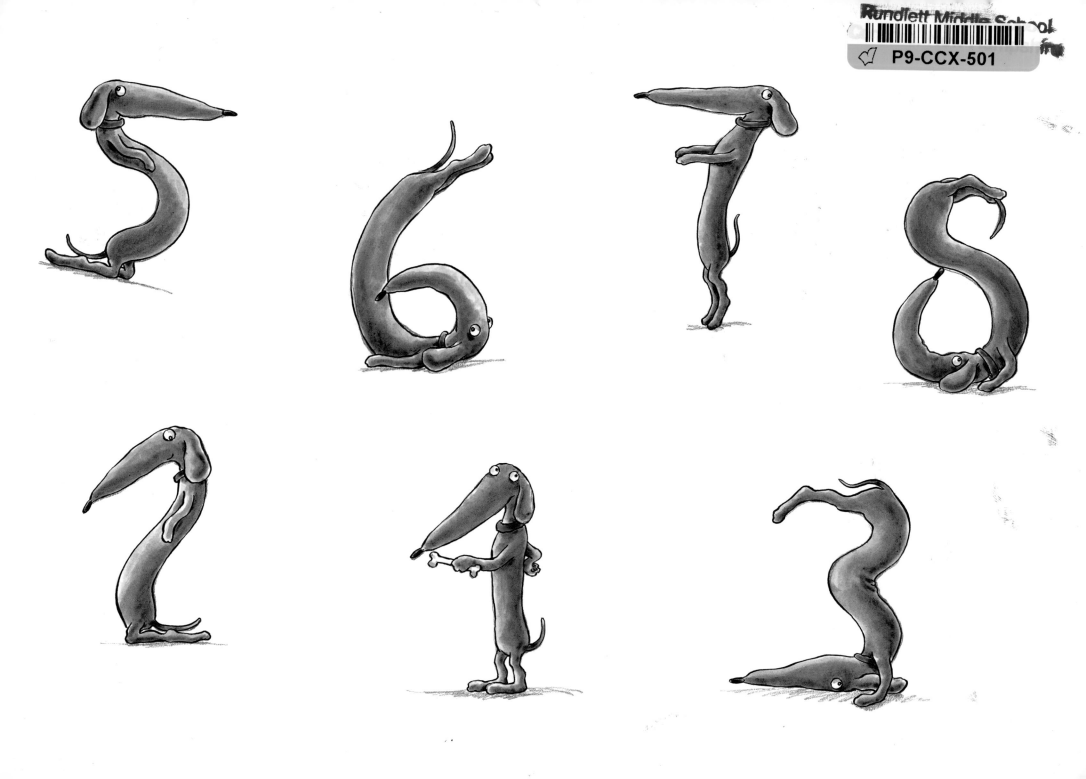

E
513.2
GRE

#A38243

Caroline Grégoire was born in 1970 in Namur, Belgium and currently lives in Spa. Her enthusiasm for children's books, painting and color led her to her career as an author, illustrator and graphic designer. **Counting with Apollo** is her second book featuring the amusing and adorable Apollo.

First American Edition 2004 by Kane/Miller Book Publishers
La Jolla, California

Originally published in 1999 in Germany under the title Apollo, rundrum schön gezählt!
Copyright ©1999 by Baumhaus Buchverlag GmbH, Frankfurt am Main (Germany).

All rights reserved. For information contact:
Kane/Miller Book Publishers
P.O. Box 8515
La Jolla, CA 92038-8515
www.kanemiller.com

Library of Congress Control Number: 2003109288

Printed and bound in China by Regent Publishing Services Ltd.

1 2 3 4 5 6 7 8 9 10

ISBN 1-929132-58-1

Counting with

Caroline Grégoire

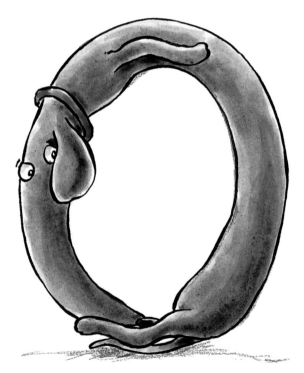

Kane/Miller
BOOK PUBLISHERS

Have you met my
best friend Apollo?

Apollo is adorable.

Apollo is also very amusing, very kind and very clever. He can teach you how to count to 10.

Pay close attention!

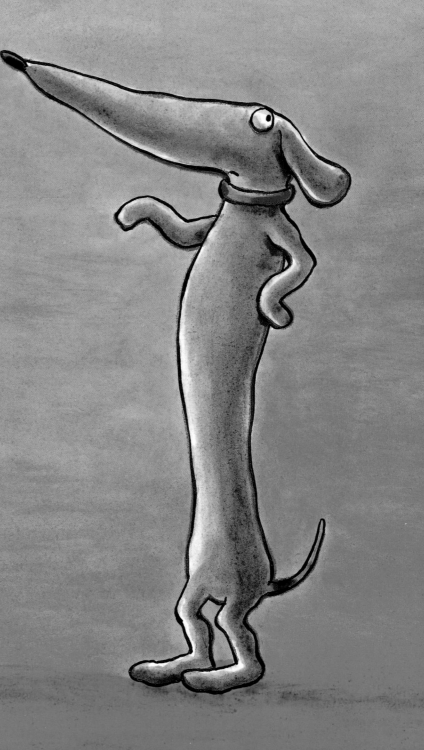

Apollo has **one** beautiful tail,
which looks like a little sausage.
He wags it when he is happy.

1

He has **two** beautiful ears,
and **two** beautiful eyes.

2

3

If Apollo only had **three** legs, it would be very impractical. He'd have to hop everywhere.

That's why Apollo has *four* legs.

4

Because he has four legs, Apollo can run faster than the neighbor's cats...the neighbor has *five* cats!

5

Naturally, Apollo does have his faults.
He can't stand cats.

And sometimes he eats too much – like eating *six* bones at once.

6

Sometimes he even eats **seven** bones.

7

Other times he is very silly, and he eats **eight** bones!

8

The worst is when he eats
nine bones!
What a catastrophe!
When he overeats, he tries
to pretend that nothing
has happened.

9

Apollo knows he shouldn't eat so many bones. He will try to cover it up by smiling his most beautiful smile. So, now you can count his *ten* teeth.

10

He really is very naughty. I don't have to scold him though, because when he has eaten too many bones poor old Apollo gets very sick.

First he turns **yellow**...

...and then **green.**

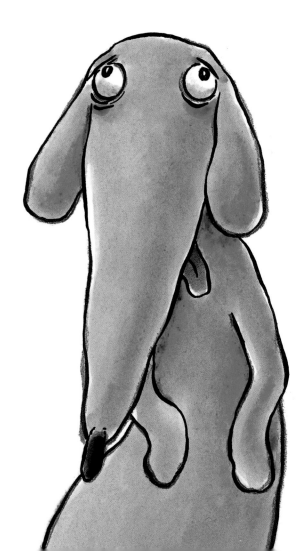

...then **purple**

Sometimes he turns **blue**...

...quite often

...and once he even
turned **grey!**

he turns **red**...

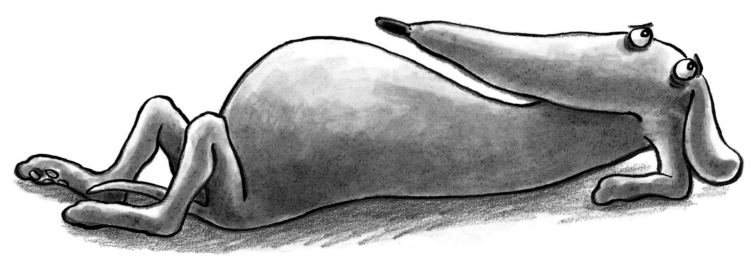

Then, after a while, he turns back into my old friend Apollo.

He promises me he will never overeat again.
He will simply use all of his energy – and all of his body – to help you learn to count from 1 to 10.

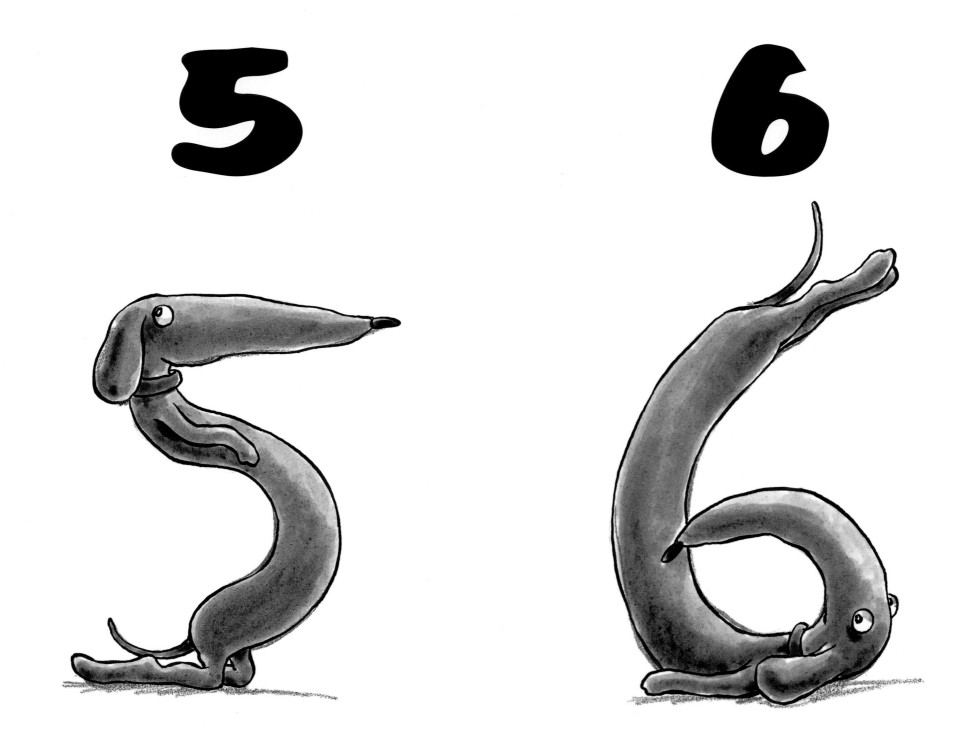

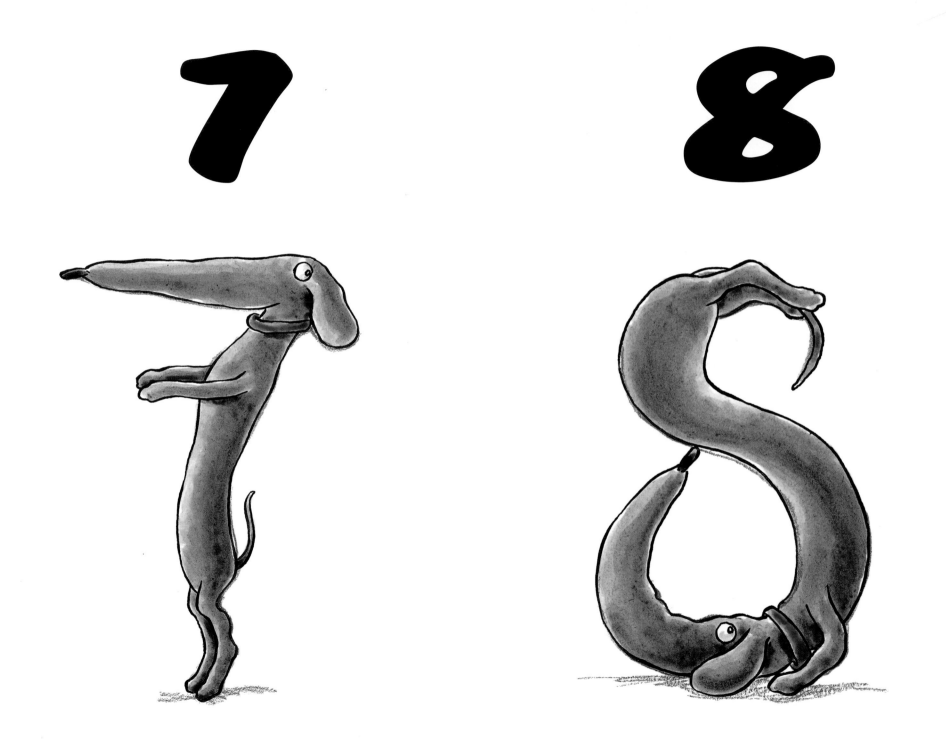

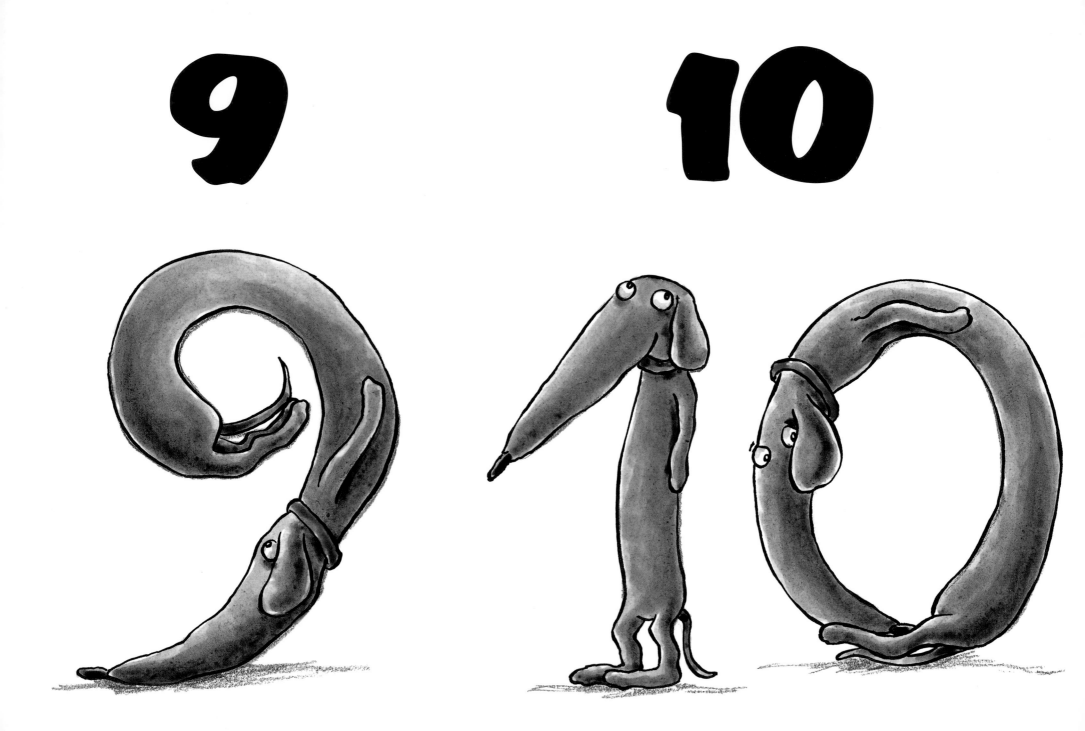

Good job, **Apollo!**

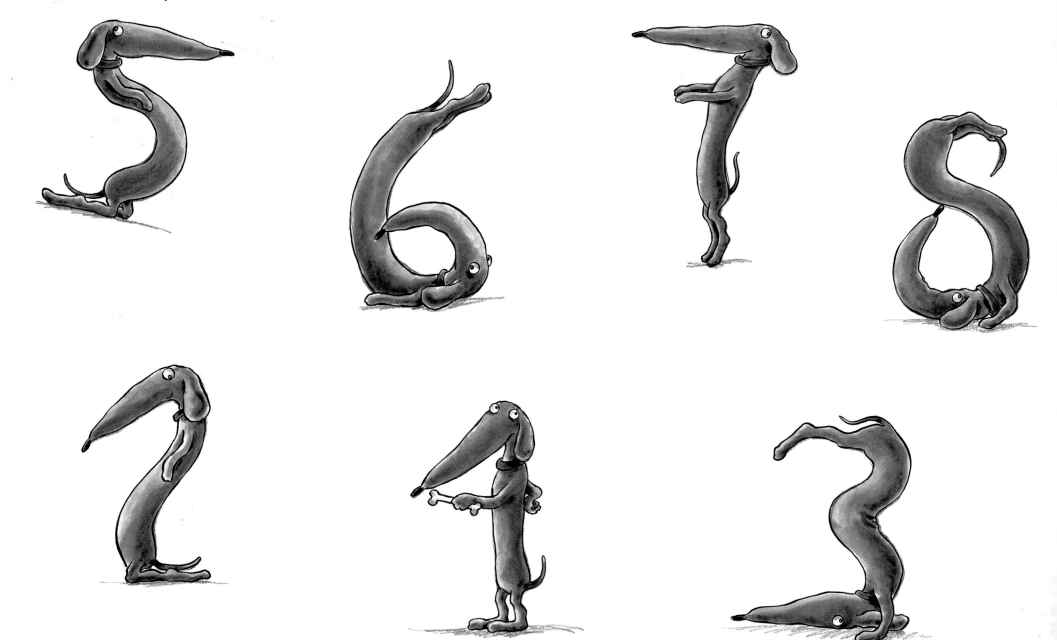